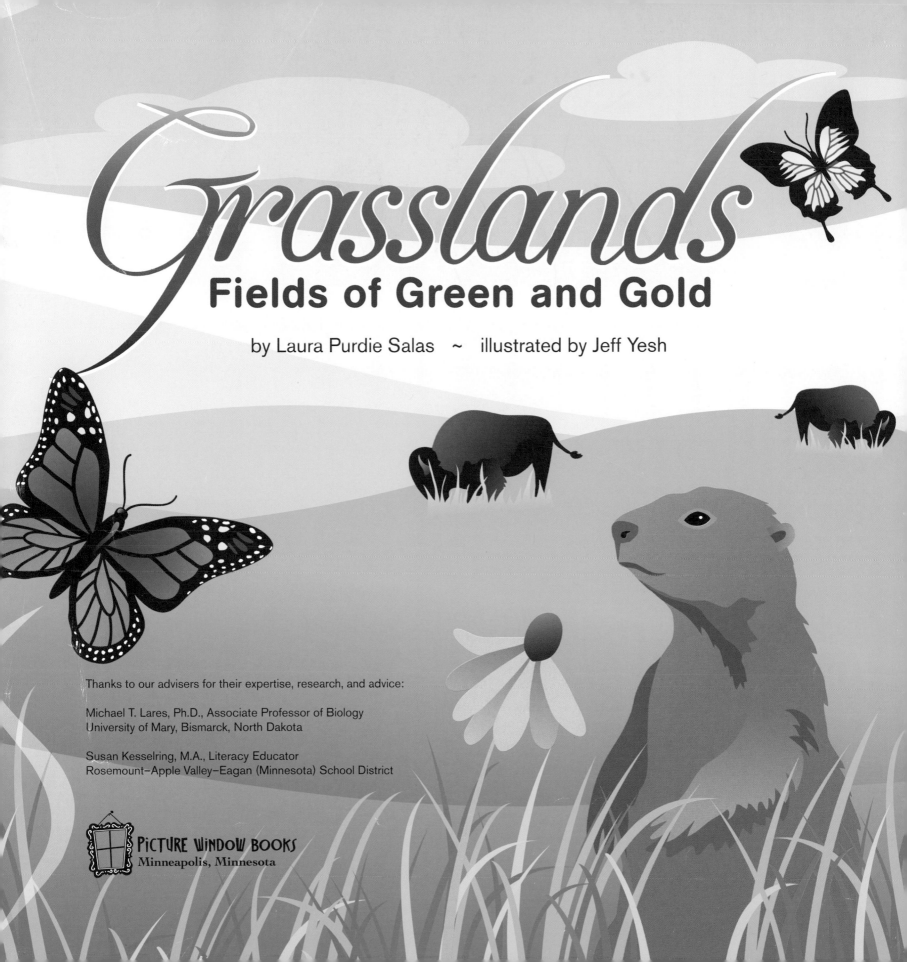

Grasslands
Fields of Green and Gold

by Laura Purdie Salas ~ illustrated by Jeff Yesh

Thanks to our advisers for their expertise, research, and advice:

Michael T. Lares, Ph.D., Associate Professor of Biology
University of Mary, Bismarck, North Dakota

Susan Kesselring, M.A., Literacy Educator
Rosemount–Apple Valley–Eagan (Minnesota) School District

PICTURE WINDOW BOOKS
Minneapolis, Minnesota

Editor: Jill Kalz

Designers: Joe Anderson and Hilary Wacholz

Page Production: Angela Kilmer

Art Director: Nathan Gassman

Associate Managing Editor: Christianne Jones

The illustrations in this book were created digitally.

Picture Window Books

5115 Excelsior Boulevard

Suite 232

Minneapolis, MN 55416

877-845-8392

www.picturewindowbooks.com

Printed in the United States of America.

Library of Congress Cataloging-in-Publication Data

Salas, Laura Purdie.

Grasslands : fields of green and gold / by Laura Purdie Salas ;
illustrated by Jeff Yesh.

p. cm. – (Amazing science)

Includes bibliographical references and index.

ISBN-13: 978-1-4048-3096-7 (library binding)

ISBN-10: 1-4048-3096-0 (library binding)

ISBN-13: 978-1-4048-3470-5 (paperback)

ISBN-10: 1-4048-3470-2 (paperback)

1. Grasslands–Juvenile literature. I. Yesh, Jeff, 1971– II. Title.

QH87.7.S25 2006

578.74–dc22   2006027214

Table of Contents

Wide, Open Lands

Flat, open land lies all around. Trees stand here and there. Mostly there is grass—gold and green grass. Zebras and giraffes graze. Lions sleep in the sun. Birds of all colors and sizes soar overhead.

This is a grassland ecosystem. An ecosystem is all of the living and nonliving things in a certain area. It includes plants, animals, water, soil, weather … everything!

FUN FACT

Grass height depends upon how much rain a grassland gets. Drier grasslands have very short grass. Wetter grasslands may have grass up to 12 feet (3.6 meters) tall—higher than a regular basketball hoop!

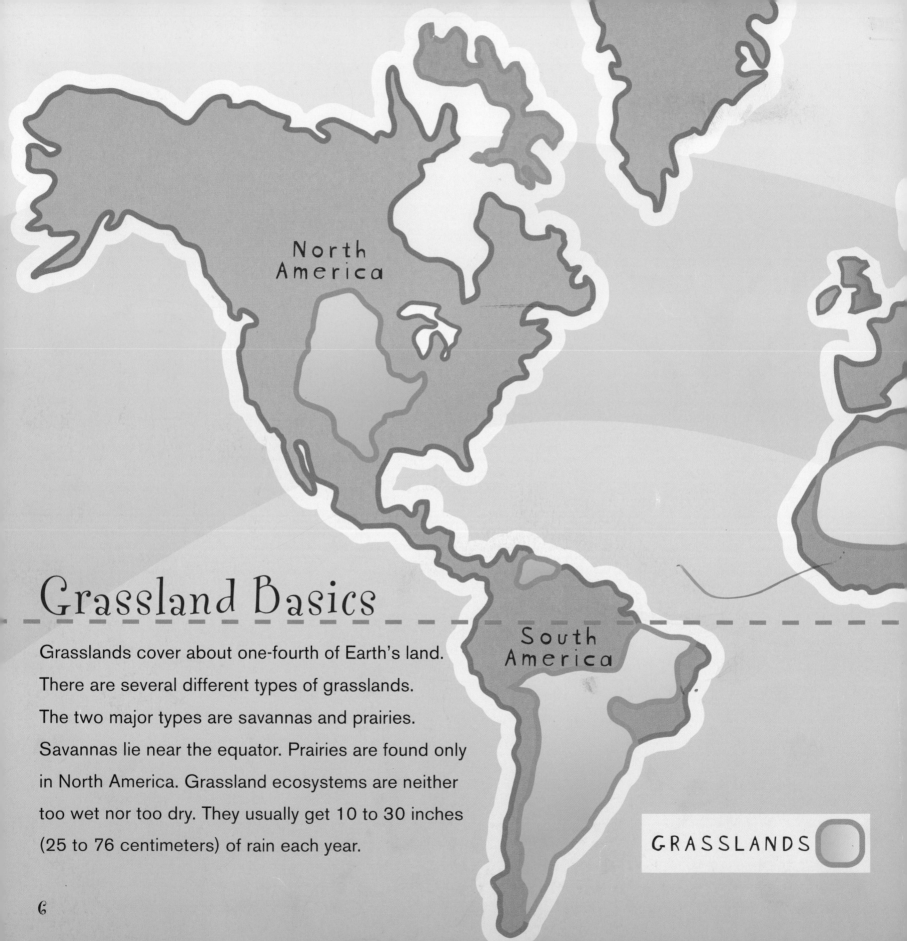

North
America

Grassland Basics

Grasslands cover about one-fourth of Earth's land.
There are several different types of grasslands.
The two major types are savannas and prairies.
Savannas lie near the equator. Prairies are found only
in North America. Grassland ecosystems are neither
too wet nor too dry. They usually get 10 to 30 inches
(25 to 76 centimeters) of rain each year.

South
America

GRASSLANDS

Asia

Europe

Africa

EQUATOR

Australia

FUN FACT

Grassland wildfires are common during the dry season. The ground is so dry that a lightning bolt can start a fire. But fire is important to the grasslands. The ash from the fire soaks into the ground when it rains. The ash helps feed the plant roots.

Savannas

Savannas lie near the equator, so they are always warm. They have a very long dry season in the winter, when little rain falls. The grasses dry up and turn yellow or brown. But then the short summer rainy season comes. Rain soaks the ground and turns the savannas green.

FUN FACT

Most animals on the savanna migrate, or move, to find water. When there is not enough rain, watering holes dry up. Millions of animals follow the rains through Africa. They migrate almost all year long.

African savannas are the largest and best-known savannas in the world. They also have the largest variety of grassland animals.

Prairies

Unlike savannas, prairies do not have rainy and dry seasons. They have hot and cold seasons, instead. They get rain or snow all year long.

Found only in North America, prairies have rich, dark soil. It is often several feet deep, which makes it easy for grasses to grow. All life on the prairie depends on these grasses.

FUN FACT

Prairies are known as the "breadbaskets of the world." Most prairie lands are now farms. The farms grow wheat, oats, and barley. Breads and cereals are made from these grains.

Grassland Animals: Grazers

Many grassland animals eat grass and other plants. These animals are called grazers. On the prairies, grazers include bison and elk. Zebras, wildebeests, and gazelles are examples of grazers on the African savannas. Grazers often feed in large herds while a few lookouts stand guard. If the guard animals see danger coming, they signal the rest of the group to run away.

FUN FACT

Tens of millions of bison once roamed the U.S. prairies. There were so many of these brown-haired animals living on the prairies that the prairies often looked brown. But early settlers hunted the bison until they were almost all gone. Today, the United States has about 350,000 bison.

Grassland Animals: Predators

Animals that eat grazers are called predators. Common prairie predators include coyotes and wolves. Cheetahs, lions, and hyenas are common predators on the African savannas. Predators have sharp teeth and claws and are fast runners. Some of them hunt in groups. Most predators sleep during the day and hunt at night.

Predators usually catch the oldest or weakest grazers. The strong grazing animals survive longer and have more babies. This cycle helps to keep the grazing population healthier overall.

FUN FACT

Birds, bugs, and other animals also live in grasslands. So do lots of burrowing animals, such as prairie dogs, rabbits, and mice. Burrowing animals may sleep underground for the entire winter.

Grasses

What are the main plants of the grassland? Grasses, of course! Grasses are needle-shaped. Their shape allows the wind to blow right through the grasslands without harming the plants.

Most plants grow at their tips. But grasses grow from their base, or bottom. When grazers nibble, they eat the older part of the plants. That means the plants can live longer.

FUN FACT

Most grassland plants have deep roots. The roots help plants reach deep-lying water during dry seasons. They also help plants survive when freezing temperatures or wildfires damage parts of the plants above ground.

Where Are the Trees?

Grasslands don't get enough rain to grow a lot of trees. When trees do grow, wildfires and grazers often kill them. Not only do grazing animals eat small trees, their hooves beat them down, too.

Savannas have more trees than prairies do. Acacia trees are common on the African savannas. These umbrella-shaped trees have deep roots to reach water far underground. Baobab trees also grow on the African savannas. They store water between the bark and the wood in their thick trunks.

FUN FACT

Baobab trees can live several thousand years. They have very thick trunks and small, skinny branches. They can reach 75 feet (23 m) tall.

Threats to Grasslands

There used to be more grasslands in the world, with more animals. What happened?

People moved in and burned huge areas of land to plant wheat and corn. They often used poor farming methods that led to erosion. When heavy rains fell, the soil washed away. Grasses disappeared. With no food to eat, many grassland animals disappeared, too.

Grassland ecosystems are home to millions of animals and plants. It's important to protect them and all of Earth's other ecosystems, too. Each has its own special gifts. Together, Earth's ecosystems make the planet an amazing place to live!

FUN FACT

Groups of people throughout the United States are working to save the country's prairies. They are buying land, planting grasses, and keeping others from building nearby. Some grasslands have been set aside as national parks to protect them from harm.

Grassland Diorama: Grassland in a Box

WHAT YOU NEED:

- a shoebox
- a paintbrush
- scissors
- straw

- black or blue paint
- colored paper
- glue
- pictures of grassland animals, such as zebras, bison, and lions

WHAT YOU DO:

1. First, turn the shoebox on its side.

2. Do you want it to be daytime? If so, paint the sides and top inside the shoebox light blue or cover them with light blue paper. Do you want it to be night? If so, choose black paint (or paper) instead. Make a paper sun or moon in the sky.

3. Spread a thin layer of glue on the bottom of the shoebox. Place straw in the glue for grass.

4. Does your grassland have a tree or two? You decide! Draw or use pictures of animals for your grassland. Which grazers will you include? Which predators?

Grassland Facts

- Termite towers are common in Australian grasslands. Tiny, ant-like termites build mud towers that are about 5 feet (1.5 m) tall. Some towers can be as high as 18 feet (5.5 m) tall!

- Grassland predators and prey (the animals they hunt) run fast. Jackrabbits can hop 45 miles (72 kilometers) per hour. They can outrun coyotes, which run up to 40 miles (64 km) per hour. But no animal outruns a cheetah. It is the fastest land animal on Earth. It can run short distances at 70 miles (113 km) per hour.

- In a grassland, 70 percent of all plant matter is below ground as roots. In a forest, only 10 percent of the plant matter is below ground.

- Prairies can be home to huge numbers of animals. One prairie dog town found in the early 20th century had an estimated 400 million prairie dogs living in it!

Glossary

ecosystem–an area with certain animals, plants, weather, and land or water features

equator–an imaginary line around the middle of Earth; it divides the northern half from the southern half

erosion–when soil is worn away by water or wind

grazers–animals that eat grasses and other plants

migrate–to travel to find food, water, warmer weather, or a place to give birth

predators–animals that hunt and eat other animals

To Learn More

AT THE LIBRARY

Bullock, Linda. *Living in the Savannah.* Danbury, Conn.: Children's Press, 2004.

Sievert, Terri. *Prairie Plants.* Mankato, Minn.: Bridgestone Books, 2006.

Stille, Darlene R. *Grasslands.* New York: Children's Press, 1999.

Wilkins, Sally. *Grasslands.* Mankato, Minn.: Bridgestone Books, 2001.

ON THE WEB

FactHound offers a safe, fun way to find Web sites related to this book. All of the sites on FactHound have been researched by our staff.

1. Visit *www.facthound.com*
2. Type in this special code: 1404830960
3. Click on the FETCH IT button.

Your trusty FactHound will fetch the best sites for you!

Index

LOOK FOR ALL OF THE BOOKS IN THE AMAZING SCIENCE– ECOSYSTEMS SERIES:

Deserts: Thirsty Wonderlands
Grasslands: Fields of Green and Gold
Oceans: Underwater Worlds
Rain Forests: Gardens of Green
Temperate Deciduous Forests: Lands of Falling Leaves
Wetlands: Soggy Habitat